WISCONSIN

A PICTURE BOOK TO REMEMBER HER BY

Designed by
DAVID GIBBON

Produced by
TED SMART

CRESCENT BOOKS
NEW YORK

INTRODUCTION

Lying between Lake Michigan to the east and the Upper Mississippi River to the west, Wisconsin, one of the north central states of the U.S.A. is bounded by Lake Superior to the north, Iowa and Minnesota to the southwest and west, and Illinois to the south. Its basic topography reveals gentle, rolling landscape covering the southern two-thirds of the state and beautiful forests, with a myriad of lakes in its northern border.

Wisconsin became the 30th member of the Union in 1848, but its history began over 200 years earlier with its discovery by the French explorer Jean Nicolet, who had been sent by Samuel de Champlain, Governor of New France, to search for the fabled Northwest Passage to Cathay. When Nicolet landed at Green Bay in 1634, so convinced was he that he had reached his destination, he donned a robe of Chinese damask and prepared to step ashore on Oriental soil. Met by the native Indians, who were doubtless amazed at the sight of this extraordinary white man, it was immediately obvious that the expedition was not in China! Yet, whilst the French did not discover the treasure and riches which Marco Polo had written of, they did find wealth of another kind – fur – and so began the fur trade that was to be of paramount importance over the next two centuries.

As the fur trapping trade increased in value, violence broke out between the French, who controlled the territory, and the British, who gained possession in 1763, at the end of the French and Indian War. Ceded to the United States by the Treaty of Paris in 1783, which marked the end of the American Revolution, hostilities now continued between the Indians and Americans, until the Black Hawk War of 1832 culminated in the final defeat of the Indian Chief and his Sauk braves who were dispossessed of their land.

The 1830s saw a great influx of immigrants from Northern Europe who were attracted by the lucrative American Fur Company, and Wisconsin's natural resources. Swedes and Finns settled in the forested areas, Germans and Danes in the potentially good farming land between Sheboygan and Racine, and the Swiss in the south central region, whilst the potato famine in Ireland, a decade later, brought large numbers of Irish to the lead mining and farming areas. Names such as Rhinelander, Eau Claire and Lake Geneva recall the state's early, mixed settlers.

With the important lead interests, which had much to do with the organization of Wisconsin Territory in 1836, lumbering, and developing agriculture, initially in wheat farming, followed by diversified farming and dairying, the state prospered. Stories of Wisconsin's mythical hero, the gigantic lumberjack Paul Bunyan and his companions, Babe the Blue Ox and Johnny Inkslinger, abounded. He was credited not only with the shaping of Wisconsin's lakes and forests, but was also said to have created the Grand Canyon, Puget Sound and the Black Hills!

By the 1870s the lumbering frontier had reached the state's north woods and exploitation was to continue for another forty years, devastating the countryside. In an effort to restore this, one of the state's most valuable assets, a forestry commission was hastily founded and, with re-forestation and the establishment of a tourist-recreation industry, the area is rapidly recovering.

With the intensified slavery issue came the formation of a new political party in 1854, the Republicans, who were to receive the majority vote until 1932. The Progressive movement, brought about by the political unrest which had been brewing since the end of the Civil War, brought the reformer Robert M. La Follette Snr. to the forefront, and the resulting passage of bills made Wisconsin a state leader in social legislation. The effort to unite the university, citizens' groups and the resources of the state government in a joint effort to solve political, economic and social problems became known as the 'Wisconsin Idea' of 1900.

Although Madison is the State Capital, Milwaukee is the largest city and centre of trade in Wisconsin. First visited by French missionaries in the late 17th century it was founded as a trading post in 1795 by Jacques Vieau. Its early growth and cultural development was strongly influenced by German settlers, and the late 1890s saw large influxes of Poles and Italians. The city is renowned for its particularly fine harbour on Lake Michigan, which is open most of the year, and accessible to the largest ships using the Great Lakes-St Lawrence Seaway, with coal and grain being the most important commodities handled there. An important industrial centre, its manufacturing industries include those of metals, machinery and consumer goods, whilst its three leading brewery headquarters have earned for the city the reputation of 'beer capital of the world'.

Madison, located in the south central part of the state, was founded in 1863 and named in honour of President James Madison. Its steady growth was encouraged first by the efforts of Leonard J. Farwell, who championed industrial growth, and by the introduction of the railroad in 1854. A prosperous city, it is characterised by landscaped lakeshores, beautiful parks and a skyline dominated by one of the nation's most impressive Capitol Buildings.

Today this attractive state which has carefully maintained an excellent balance between its agricultural and manufacturing interests, has also developed its magnificent natural resources which draw countless vacationers to its varied landscape. Throughout the state Wisconsin's fine system of parks and forests preserve a wealth of unusual scenic splendour and fascinating historic sites. One of the most outstanding is the picturesque Dells area of the Wisconsin River, where fantastic rock formations, carved through the soft sandstone by the river over a distance of 15 miles, can be seen by special river-trips through the Upper and Lower Dells. With a host of recreational opportunities, evidenced in the unique Door County Peninsula; beautiful Lake Michigan shores; majestic northern lakes region offering forest trails, and clear streams and lakes for fishing and canoeing, and popular winter sports, Wisconsin is certainly one of the country's most appealing vacation states.

Colourful wildflowers bloom in profusion along Highway 17, north of Rhinelander *left*.

Milwaukee *above,* the second largest city and commercial metropolis of Wisconsin, is sited on the west shore of Lake Michigan. In the Downtown area, seen from Water Street Bridge *overleaf* and reflected in the lake's dark waters *bottom left,* is located the Performing Arts Center *right and centre left. Top left* is shown McKinley Marina, and *below* small boats becalmed at their moorings by night.

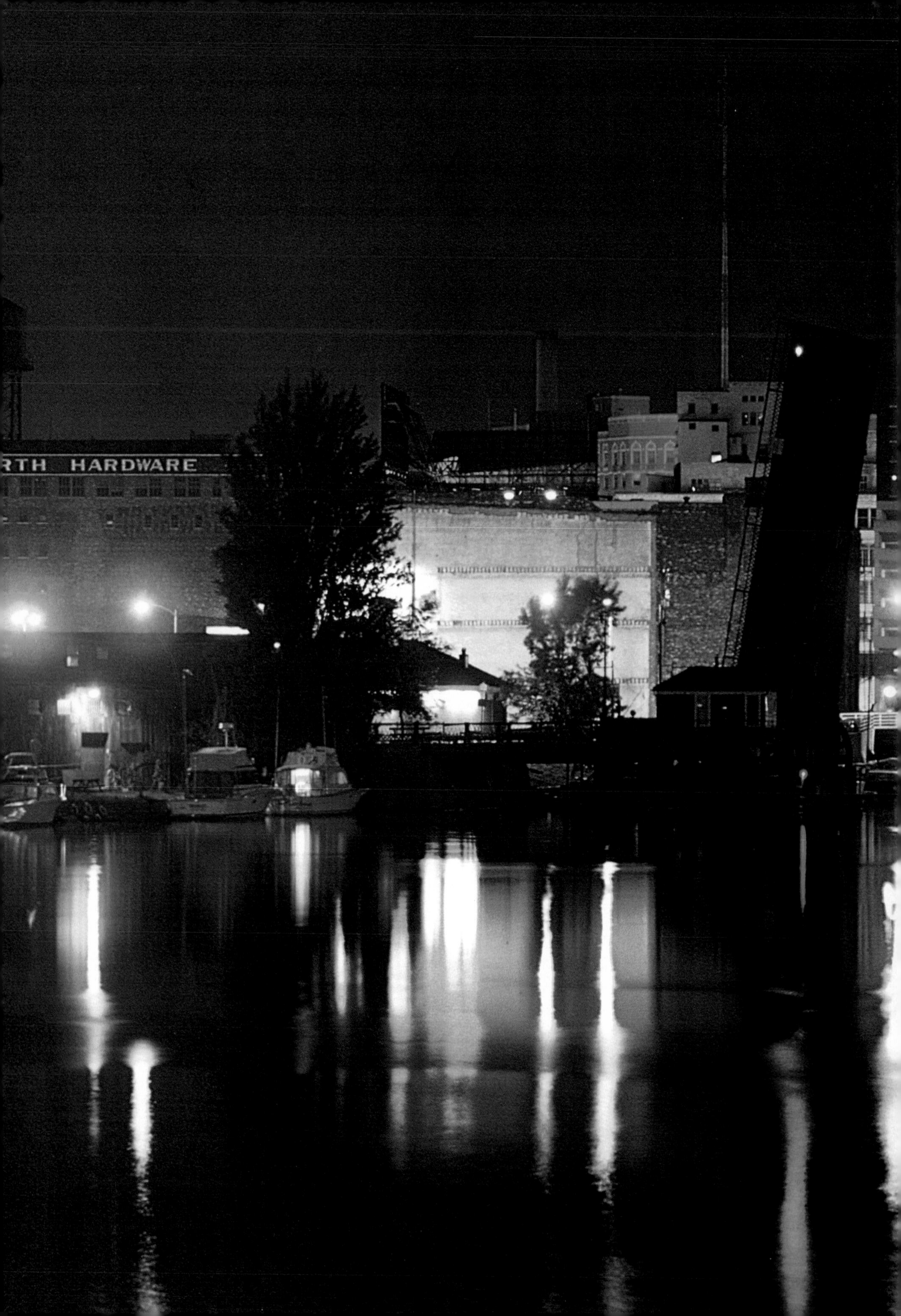
RTH HARDWARE

On view in the Milwaukee Art Center are the painting and sculpture exhibits *top, centre and bottom right; top* is shown the lavish interior of The Pabst Theater; *above* symbolistic sculpture gracing the exterior of The Performing Arts Center; *below* the Old North Point Water Tower and *left* neon-lit Wisconsin Avenue.

Beautiful floral displays are a particular feature of The Boerner Botanical Gardens *above*, in Whitnall Park, and *left* can be seen The Miller Brewing Company, one of three great brewing headquarters in this famous 'beer capital of the world'. Of special historic interest is City Hall, the interior of which is shown *below*, one of Milwaukee's noted public buildings, whilst *right*, highlighting lovely Plankington Arcade, is the statue of John Plankington, one of the city's early entrepreneurs.

Summerfest *these pages*, with over fifty events, including a circus, amusement rides, various music programmes and sporting events, is a ten-day family entertainment attraction which takes place at Milwaukee's waterfront in early July.

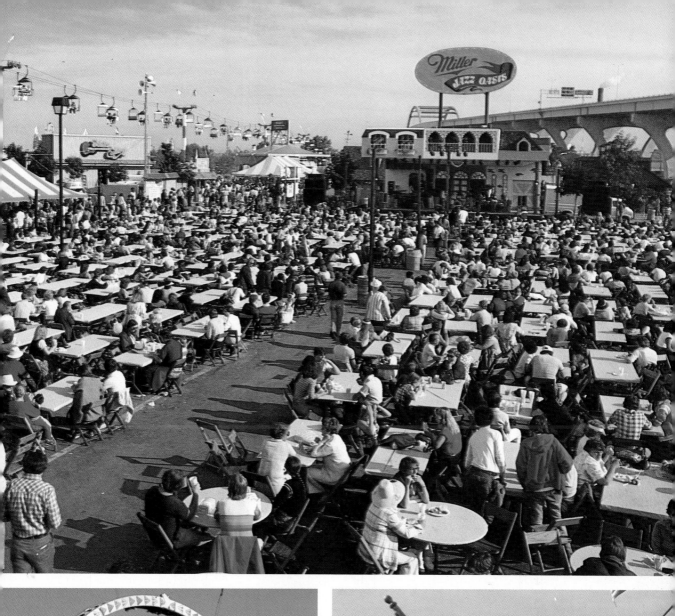

Amongst Milwaukee's magnificent shrines of worship are: the Tripoli Mosque *top*, with its exquisite domed lobby *left;* the St Joan of Arc Chapel *above*, a 15th century French chapel first rebuilt on Long Island and presented to the Marquette University in 1964; Frank Lloyd Wright's Annunciation Greek Orthodox Church *bottom left*, and the St Josaphat Basilica, with its sumptuous interior *right.* Of Flemish-Renaissance architecture, the exterior of City Hall is shown *below*, and *overleaf* the National Square Dancers Convention in the city's Convention Center.

14

"Major League" when it comes to sport, Milwaukee is home of the Brewers baseball team, seen in play versus the Chicago Whitesox at the County Stadium *above and near right*. Shown *top, centre and bottom left*, and *below*, as A. J. Foyt takes the winner's trophy, are scenes from the Rex Mays Classic which brings the Indy 500 drivers to the State Fair Park in mid-June. The smooth greens of Whitnall Park Golf Course can be seen *far right*.

One of Milwaukee's most distinctive landmarks, The Mitchell Park Horticultural Conservatory, features three conoidal glass domes *above, bottom and right*, each 85 feet high and 140 feet wide, which, with separate, artificially controlled climates, display exotic, tropical blooms, unusual desert specimens and changing, seasonal flowers.

Brown bears *left*, giraffes *below left* and elephants *below*, in natural habitat settings, can be seen in the internationally acclaimed Milwaukee County Zoo.

Door County, one of the most unusual
vacationlands in the Great Lakes region, is
lapped on its eastern shore by Lake
Michigan and by Green Bay on its western,
where islands, bays, harbours and bluffs
have been carved by the Bay's deep waters.

A popular fishing area throughout the
summer until late autumn, anglers can take
trout in April, which sees the start of the
season, pike and bass during the mid-
summer months and trout and chinook
salmon in November, whilst in the winter
months the county is also a noted ski and
snowmobile centre.

Across the Strait of Death's Door *right*, at
the northern tip of the peninsula, where
the picturesque community of Gills Rock
top left is sited, lies Washington Island, a
favourite summer resort area. South of
Sturgeon Bay, which bisects the peninsula,
is located Algoma *above* and Kewaunee
centre left, on the shores of beautiful
Lake Michigan.

Isolated farms, nestling amid the lush,
green pastureland south of Kewaunee, can
be seen along Highway 42 *left*.

23

Revealing the scenic vacationland of Central Wisconsin's River Country is the Wisconsin River, seen at Stevens Point *left and top right;* a tranquil sunset over the still lake at Whiting *centre right* and the peaceful roadside pond south of Wisconsin Rapids *above.* Detailing the history of the famous Grand Rapids *bottom right* is the plaque *bottom,* and *below* is shown the lovely City Hall at Two Rivers in Manitowoc County.

GRAND RAPIDS
OF THE WISCONSIN RIVER

Indians called this section of the river "Ahdawagam" -- the two sided rapids, while lumbermen knew it as "Grand Rapids"--the most treacherous stretch of the river, accentuated by perilous Sherman Rock. Bloomer, Sampson and Strong harnessed the waterpower in 1838 for sawing lumber. The abundant waterpower resulted in other mills being built and communities developed on each bank of the river. Centralia on the west bank and Grand Rapids on the east side were united in 1900 as Grand Rapids and later renamed Wisconsin Rapids.

Ferries spanned the river until a wooden toll bridge was built in 1867, only to be washed out in 1888. On several occasions, the Grand Rapids have been unable to cope with the ice and flood waters with devastating floods resulting; the worst of these being in 1880 and 1935. The flow of water in 1935 reached a record half million gallons per second, accompanied by the cry, "The Biron Dam has gone out."

The last lumber raft passed over the rapids in 1887. In 1901 the numerous waterpower developments on both sides of the river were combined into one company known as Consolidated Water Power Company, a parent company of the present paper mill on the opposite bank of the river. Thus lumbering gave way to papermaking.

Erected 1964

In the picturesque Dells region of the Wisconsin River, where fantastic rock forms have been carved by the River over a distance of 15 miles, can be seen the mysterious canyons, creviced gorges and intriguing rock formations *these pages*.

Broadway *right* is located in the picturesque town of Wisconsin Dells, seen in a superb aerial view *above*, which contains a host of attractions, including Riverview Park *centre left*, a popular fun spot for all the family. *Top left and below* can be seen the Wisconsin River as it winds through the thickly forested area of the lovely Dells region, and *bottom left* Circus World Museum at Baraboo.

Madison, capital of Wisconsin, contains one of the nation's most impressive State Capitol Buildings. With a sumptuously decorated interior *left,* the majestic Capitol can be seen *above left* reflected in the glossy exterior of the First Wisconsin Plaza Building.

Sited on spring-fed Lake Geneva is the noted year-round resort of Lake Geneva *top right, above and below.* The resort boasts a host of recreational facilities, including those of the popular Playboy Club *top, centre and bottom right.*

One of the charming log buildings in the unique outdoor museum of Little Norway, nestled in the beautiful Valley of the Elves, The Norway Building *right and above* is a perfect example of authentic Norse architecture.

Originally founded in 1861, Mount Horeb, a delightful Scandinavian community with a strong cultural heritage and fascinating gift shops *left*, is today a thriving village set amid prosperous dairy farms.

Calm and still, the flooded Wisconsin River *below* is pictured on the outskirts of Boydtown, Crawford County.

Built on a sixty foot chimney rock in the heart of The Uplands Country, the incredible House on the Rock, with its fascinating, sumptuously furnished rooms *these pages* and The Streets of Yesterday *top left,* is one of the midwest's top tourist attractions, which was created by Alex Jordan and opened to the public in 1961.

Set amid beautifully landscaped grounds, the Villa Louis at Prairie du Chien is shown *above; right* the superb vista from Point Lookout, Wyalusing State Park, revealing the Meeting of the Wisconsin and Mississippi Rivers; *top left* a tranquil scene outside Lynxville *centre left; bottom left* Riverside Park at La Crosse and *overleaf* a dramatic sunset over Grandad Bluff.

RAFTING ON THE MISSISSIPPI

After 1837 the vast timber resources of northern Wisconsin were eagerly sought by settlers moving into the mid-Mississippi valley. By 1847 there were more than thirty saw-mills on the Wisconsin, Chippewa and St. Croix river systems, cutting largely Wisconsin white pine.

During long winter months, logging crews felled and stacked logs on the frozen rivers. Spring thaws flushed the logs down the streams toward the Mississippi River. Here logs were caught, sorted, scaled and rafted. Between 1837 and 1901 more than forty million board feet of logs floated down the Great River to saw-mills.

The largest log raft on the Mississippi was assembled at Lynxville in 1896. It was 270 feet wide and 1550 long, containing two and one-fourth million board feet of lumber.

The largest lumber raft on the river originated on Lake St. Croix in 1901. Somewhat smaller in size, 270 feet wide and 1450 feet long, it carried more lumber, nine million board feet. The last rafting of lumber on the Mississippi came in 1915, ending a rich, exciting and colorful era in the history of Wisconsin and the Great River.

Erected 1965

Farms and acres of arable farmland dot the fertile countryside of this wide and varied state where agriculture is basic to the economy. North of Chippewa Falls, which has developed as a trading centre for dairying and agricultural products, are the picturesque farms *top left, right, below and overleaf.* Shown *top* is a farm at Galesville, north of La Crosse; *centre left and below left* the lovely scenery in Lake Wissota State Park, which covers 1,044 acres, five miles east of Chippewa Falls, whilst *bottom* can be seen a fisherman proudly displaying his catch of wall eye pike.

40

With a wealth of State Parks and beautiful recreation areas, the state offers a magnificent variety of unrivalled scenery. The Chippewa River cascades over Jim Falls to flow along a boulder-strewn bed *top left;* towering conifers are reflected in the majestic waters of one of 400 lakes that dot the extensive Chequamegon National Forest *centre left,* and *right* can be seen the leafy greenery of the Hartman Creek State Park near Waupaca. In the Rib Mountain State Park, one of the midwest's finest ski areas, can be seen the park's highest point of elevation, at 1,940 feet *above,* and *below* the County Marker near Brunet Island State Park, recounts the fascinating history of 'Old Abe', The War Eagle. Under a cloudless sky pretty dairyfarms are shown near Lake Wissota *bottom left* and on the outskirts of Boyd *overleaf.*

OLD ABE, THE WAR EAGLE

This wayside is part of the old McCann farm, childhood home of Old Abe, the War Eagle. In the Spring of 1861 a band of hungry Chippewa came to the McCann farm and traded a young eagle for corn. The eagle became a family pet. When Company C, Eighth Wisconsin was organized at Eau Claire for Civil War duty, the crippled Dan McCann offered his eagle's services as mascot, feeling that "someone from the family ought to go." On October 12, 1861, the Eagle Regiment started for the front. In action Old Abe spread his wings and screamed encouragement to his men. The louder the noise of battle, the louder and fiercer were his screams. The eagle served with the regiment in 42 skirmishes and battles and lost only a few feathers. After three years' service, Old Abe was formally presented to the State of Wisconsin September 26, 1864. A room was equipped for him in the Capitol and a man employed to care for him. His last public appearance occurred at the National Encampment of the G.A.R. in Milwaukee in 1880, where he and General U.S. Grant were honored guests. After a brief illness, Old Abe died March 28, 1881.

In contrast to the tranquillity of the Hartman Creek State Park *above and below left*, is the excitement of 'running the rapids' on the Big Smoky Falls of the Wolf River *below and right*, which also provides excellent canoeing facilities at Markton *above*.

Rhinelander, with its graceful County Courthouse *below,* and crowded Brown Street *below left,* originated in the late nineteenth century during the days of the pioneer lumber industry and today boasts one of the largest paper mills in America. North of the city can be seen the massed banks of flowers *top left and right,* which flood the roadside with colour along Highway 17, and *above* small boys fish in the silver waters of Lake Metonga at Crandon.

Thrilling stagecoach rides *left and right*, gold-panning *below*, and a host of exciting activities, including horseback riding, go-kart racing, trout fishing and little river boat rides, are part of the numerous attractions at Eagle Pass Park's Pleasure Island, sited one mile north of Eagle River in the Northwoods territory. This authentic 1880's Western Town *above* recaptures the stirring days of early pioneer life and features gunfights and train robberies, as well as special performances by the Birdcage Theater Show and animated three ring circus. Guests can also see a number of Northwoods' animals at close quarters and pet and feed the tame deer in the park.

Sentinel straight, the bright-tinted wild lupins line Highway 13, north of Washburn *overleaf*.

53

The spectacular Cascades *above*, Brownstone Falls *overleaf* and meandering Bad River *bottom right* are part of the scenic wonderland of Copper Falls State Park.

Nestled in the hills along Chequamegon Bay is the picturesque fishing village of Bayfield with its carefully preserved Victorian house *below* and elegant Old Rittenhouse Inn *top right*.

A gaily painted barn, north of Washburn, is pictured *centre right*, and *left* beautiful Arrowhead Lake, near Woodruff.

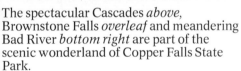

MADELINE ISLAND

Known to the Ojibway Indian as
Moningwunakauning,
"The Home of The Golden Breasted Woodpecker"

The largest of the Apostle Islands
was one of the earliest areas of
Indian settlement. fur trade. missionary
activity and commercial fishing in
the interior of North America. --
It was discovered by French ex-
plorers in 1659. Trading posts were
built here for the French by
Le Sueur in 1693 and for the British
by Michel Cadotte in 1793. In 1834
this site and present La Pointe
dock became headquarters for the
Northern Outfit of the American Fur
Company. -- Missionary operations
began about 1830 with the erection
of a Protestant Church followed by
Father Baraga's Catholic Church.

Erected by
Madeline Island Historical Museum

Madeline Island, surrounded by the
beautiful blue waters of Lake Superior, is
reached by car ferry *top left,* which, leaving
from Bayfield, docks at one of the state's
oldest settlements, La Pointe. This historic
town is noted for the Madeline Island
Historical Museum *below,* the interior of
which *centre left,* contains artifacts
relating to the history of the area,
documented on the marker *above,* as well
as the Indian Cemetery, detailed *bottom*
and lovely marina *bottom left.* Big Bay
State Park, one of the Island's newest
developments, is pictured *right and
overleaf.*

LA POINTE INDIAN CEMETERY

Established about 1836 as part of a Roman Catholic mission
under the guidance of the dynamic Austrian priest. Frederick
Baraga. later made a bishop.

The white man's style of house was adopted as a grave cover
by the Christianized Ojibway (Chippewa) in his custom of
protecting both the dead and the food left with the dead. The
food gave sustenance for the 4-day journey to the Hereafter as
well as something for the spirit to leave for friends. relatives and
the poor. A defaced stone marks the grave of Great Buffalo.
principal chief of the Ojibway on Lake Superior. Chief Little
Buffalo. his Protestant son. is buried across the road and south
in a grave marked with 4 pines.

A Frenchman. Cadeau. journeyed to Lake Superior in 1671
eventually marrying an Ojibway. His grandson. Michel Cadotte.
opened a fur-trading post on this island in 1793 for the North
West Company. a post later acquired by John Jacob Astor's
American Fur Company. Michel continuing until 1823 as manager.
Here Michel Cadotte is buried and. by his side. his grandchild
Julia Mary Warren of the noted family of fur traders and scholars

CLB 1097
© 1987 Illustrations and text: Colour Library Books Ltd.,
    Guildford, Surrey, England.
Filmsetting by Acesetters Ltd., Richmond, Surrey, England.
Published 1987 by Crescent Books, distributed by Crown Publishers, Inc.
Printed and bound in Barcelona, Spain by Cronión, S.A.
ISBN 0 517 288745
h g f e d c b a

Dep. Leg. B-43484-87